AMAZING SHARKS

Collector Card

AMAZING SHARKS

Collector Card

AMAZING SHARKS

Collector Card

AMAZING SHARKS

Collector Card

Whale shark

The world's largest living shark is the size of three elephants.

SCORE

SIZE: up to 50 ft. (15m) — 9
DANGER FACTOR: low — 2
TEETH: 0.12 in. (3mm) — 2
CONSERVATION STATUS: vulnerable — 5

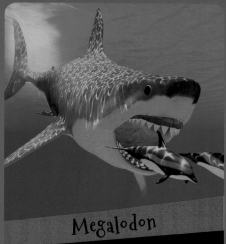

Megalodon

The prehistoric Megalodon had a mouth the size of a dining room table.

SCORE

SIZE: up to 60 ft. (18m) — 10
DANGER FACTOR: deadly — 10
TEETH: 7 in. (18cm) — 10
CONSERVATION STATUS: extinct — 0

Shortfin mako shark

The world's fastest shark can travel up to 40 mph (60km/h).

SCORE

SIZE: up to 13 ft. (4m) — 4
DANGER FACTOR: high — 7
TEETH: 1.2 in. (3cm) — 5
CONSERVATION STATUS: vulnerable — 5

Great white shark

Two-thirds of the world's shark attacks are made by great whites.

SCORE

SIZE: up to 20 ft. (6m) — 6
DANGER FACTOR: high — 9
TEETH: 2.5 in. (6.5cm) — 7
CONSERVATION STATUS: vulnerable — 5

It's all about . . .

AMAZING
SHARKS

KINGFISHER
NEW YORK

KINGFISHER
LONDON & NEW YORK

Copyright © Macmillan Publishers International Ltd 2016
Published in the United States by Kingfisher,
175 Fifth Ave., New York, NY 10010
Kingfisher is an imprint of Macmillan Children's Books, London
All rights reserved.

Distributed in the U.S. and Canada by Macmillan,
175 Fifth Ave., New York, NY 10010

Library of Congress Cataloging-in-Publication
data has been applied for.

Series editor: Sarah Snashall
Series design: Little Red Ant
Adapted from an original text by Anita Ganeri

ISBN 978-0-7534-7266-8

Kingfisher books are available for special promotions
and premiums. For details contact: Special Markets
Department, Macmillan, 175 Fifth Ave.,
New York, NY 10010.

For more information, please visit
www.kingfisherbooks.com

Printed in China

9 8 7 6 5 4 3 2 1

1TR/1115/WKT/UG/128MA

Picture credits
The Publisher would like to thank the following for permission to reproduce their material.
Top = t; Bottom = b; Center = c; Left = l; Right = r
Cover Shutterstock/Jim Agronick; background Shutterstock/PHOTOCREO Michal Bednarek;
Back cover Shutterstock/Fiona Ayerst; Pages 3 Kingfisher Artbank; 4–5 Shutterstock/Rich
Carey; 5t Shutterstock/ShaunWilkinson; 6–7 Kingfisher Artbank; 6b Shutterstock/mj007;
8–9 Kingfisher Artbank; 8 Shutterstock/Fiona Ayerst; 10–11 Shutterstock/Matt9122;
11t Naturepl/Alex Hyde; 12 Shutterstock/Joost van Uffelen; 13t FLPA/R Dirschler;
13b Shutterstock/Kjersti Joergensen; 14 Photoshot/Tony Baskeyfield/NHPA; 15 Kingfisher
Artbank; 16–17 Shutterstock/Matt9122; 17 Alamy/Jeff Rotman; 18 Shutterstock/MP cz;
19 Alamy/Charles Hood; 20 Naturepl/Doug Perrine; 21 FLPA/Flip Nicklin/Minden;
22–23 Shutterstock/Krzysztof Odziomek; 23 Shutterstock/Amanda Nicholls; 24 Shutterstock/
Sergey Uryadnikov; 25 Shutterstock/Elsa Hoffmann; 26–27 Shutterstock/Matt9122;
27tl Alamy/Peter Arnold Inc.; 27tr Shutterstock/Rich Carey; 28 Photolibrary; 29t FLPA Pete
Oxford/Minden; 29 Shutterstock/Mark William Penny; 32 Shutterstock/Fiona Ayerst.
Cards: Front tl Shutterstock/Joanne Weston; tr Shutterstock/Catmando; bl Corbis/Andy
Murch/Visuals Unlimited; br Shutterstock/Mogens Trolle; Back tl Shutterstock/A Cotton
Photo; bl Getty/Oxford Scientific; tr Naturepl/Florian Graner; br Getty/Jason Isley-Scubazoo.

Front cover: A great white shark on the look-out for food.

CONTENTS

All shapes and sizes	4
Prehistoric sharks	6
Where do sharks live?	8
Made for speed	10
Hide and seek	12
On the move	14
Shark senses	16
Scary hunters	18
Baby sharks	20
Monster shark!	22
Great white shark	24
Shark attacks	26
Sharks in danger	28
Glossary	30
Index	32

All shapes and sizes

There are more than 450 different species of shark, and they come in many shapes and sizes.

FACT...

The smallest shark is the dwarf lantern shark. It is only about the length of a pencil.

The sawshark has a flattened body and a long snout.

The mako shark has a powerful, streamlined body.

Some sharks are sleek hunters that speed through the water in search of their prey. Others, such as the whale shark, are giants that feed on tiny ocean creatures.

Prehistoric sharks

Sharks have been swimming in the oceans for more than 400 million years.

By the time the dinosaurs appeared, sharks had already been around for 200 million years!

Stethacanthus had a patch of small teeth on the top of its head and on one fin.

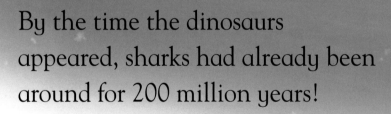

fossilized Megalodon tooth

Megalodon was a monster meat-eating shark that died out about 1.5 million years ago.

Megalodon

Stethacanthus

SPOTLIGHT: Megalodon

Record breaker: largest-ever shark

Length: up to 60 ft. (18m)

Teeth: razor sharp

Ate: whales and dolphins

Where do sharks live?

Sharks live in every part of the ocean, from the shallows to the deepest depths, and from rocky shores to coral reefs. Most are found in warm parts of the oceans. A few live in the cold oceans near the North and South poles.

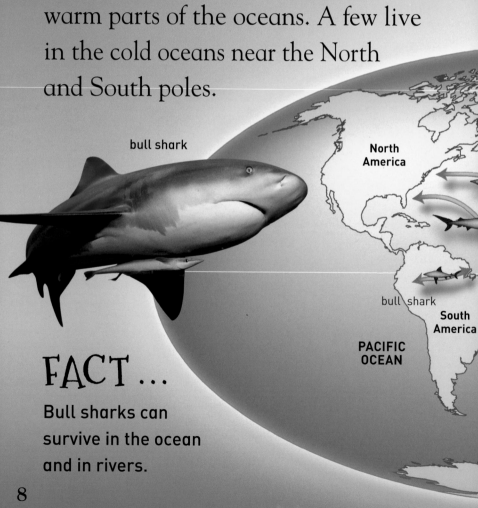

bull shark

North America

South America

PACIFIC OCEAN

bull shark

FACT ...

Bull sharks can survive in the ocean and in rivers.

In winter in the Arctic, the ocean freezes over and the Greenland shark survives underneath the ice.

Some sharks travel long distances to find food and to breed. This is called migration.

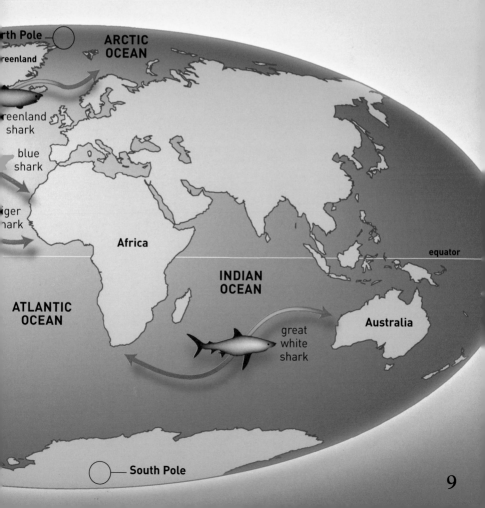

North Pole

ARCTIC OCEAN

Greenland

Greenland shark

blue shark

tiger shark

Africa

equator

INDIAN OCEAN

ATLANTIC OCEAN

great white shark

Australia

South Pole

Made for speed

Many sharks have a streamlined shape for fast swimming.

jaws—for crushing

teeth—very sharp and always growing

A shark's skeleton is not bony— it is made from rubbery cartilage. This makes the shark's body very flexible (bendy) as it swims.

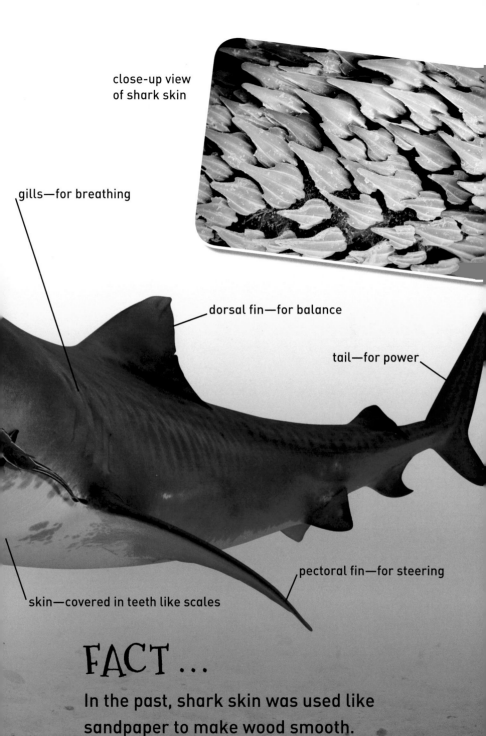

close-up view
of shark skin

gills—for breathing

dorsal fin—for balance

tail—for power

skin—covered in teeth like scales

pectoral fin—for steering

FACT...

In the past, shark skin was used like
sandpaper to make wood smooth.

11

Hide and Seek

Most sharks are ocean colored. This helps them hide from their prey. Look at this blue shark. From above, it blends in with the dark ocean floor. From below, it is hidden against the bright surface of the water.

The wobbegong lies completely still on the ocean floor waiting for a tasty fish to swim by. Its shape and colors blend in with the sand, rocks, and seaweed.

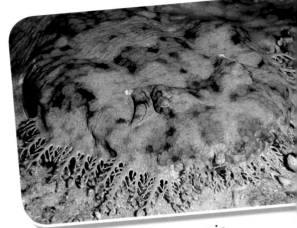

This wobbegong is perfectly hidden.

FACT ...

The spots on a leopard shark get lighter as the shark grows older.

On the move

When a shark swims, it moves its body from side to side. The shark uses its strong tail for power. It uses its fins to steer and stay upright.

SPOTLIGHT: *Shortfin mako shark*

Record breaker:	fastest shark
Length:	up to 13 ft. (4m)
Teeth:	razor sharp
Eats:	fish, squid, and other sharks

Different sharks have different-shaped tails. Some tails have evolved for fast swimming, others for cruising slowly after prey.

tiger shark

thresher shark

swell shark

Sharks have a large liver filled with oil and fat to help them float.

great white shark

FACT ...

Some sharks, such as sand tiger sharks, can store air in their stomach to help them float.

Shark senses

Sharks have very good eyesight and excellent hearing and smell. Sharks can hear sounds up to one mile (1.5 kilometers) away. Sharks can also pick up electrical signals and movement from nearby prey.

A hammerhead shark has eyes at each end of its hammer-shaped head.

Some sharks have an extra eyelid. This protects their eyes when they attack prey. Other sharks roll their eyes right back under their top eyelids.

This half-closed eye belongs to a Caribbean reef shark.

FACT...

A shark can smell blood from up to 450 yards (about 400 meters) away. They can detect one drop of blood in a million drops of water— that's enough water to fill your bathtub!

Scary hunters

Many sharks are fierce predators that hunt fish, squid, seals, dolphins, and turtles. These sharks have a large mouth lined with sharp teeth. They swallow small animals whole, or take huge bites out of bigger prey.

Many sharks have sharp teeth and powerful jaws.

Not all sharks eat in this way. Some have a huge mouth but tiny teeth. They swim along with their mouth wide open, gulping in water and filtering out tiny fish and shrimps.

The 33-feet-long (10-meter-long) basking shark swims with its huge jaws stretched wide open.

Baby sharks

Some sharks, such as blue sharks and lemon sharks, give birth to live babies, called pups.

Other sharks lay eggs in the water. The eggs have a tough case to protect them. Inside, the yolk provides food for the growing pup.

This lemon shark has just been born.

FACT...

Sometimes, empty egg cases wash up on the beach. They are known as "mermaids' purses."

Inside each of these egg cases is the embryo of a swell shark.

Monster shark!

Everything about the whale shark
is ENORMOUS! It is not only
the biggest shark, but it is also the
biggest fish in the ocean. This giant
can grow up to 50 feet (15 meters)
long and weighs as much as
three elephants.

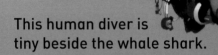
SPOTLIGHT: Whale shark

Record breaker:	largest living shark
Length:	up to 50 ft. (15m)
Teeth:	hundreds of tiny teeth
Eats:	plankton, krill, and small fish

This human diver is tiny beside the whale shark.

As a filter feeder, the whale shark swims along slowly with its mouth wide open to catch shrimps and other tiny ocean animals.

FACT …

The whale shark's mouth is lined with more than 300 rows of tiny teeth.

Great white shark

The great white shark is the largest meat-eating shark in the ocean. It is a fierce and dangerous hunter.

FACT ...

The great white shark sometimes lifts its head out of the water to see what is around it. This is called "spy-hopping."

A great white shark leaps out of the water to catch its prey.

The great white shark has jagged,
razor-sharp teeth.

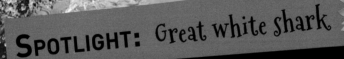

SPOTLIGHT: Great white shark

Record breaker:	largest meat-eating shark
Length:	up to 20 ft. (6m)
Teeth:	about 300 razor-sharp teeth
Eats:	fish, seals, sea lions, dolphins

Shark attacks

Some people think that all sharks are dangerous creatures that eat people. In fact, the chances of being attacked by a shark are very small. There are only about 80 shark attacks in the whole world each year, and fewer than 10 people are killed.

SPOTLIGHT: Tiger shark

Record breaker:	second most deadly to humans
Length:	about 16 ft. (5m)
Teeth:	sharp serrated teeth
Eats:	almost anything

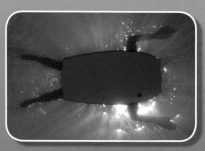

a bodyboarder

a turtle

From below, a person on a bodyboard looks just like a turtle to a hungry tiger shark.

The tiger shark will swallow almost anything it finds, including garbage.

Sharks in danger

Every year, millions of sharks die because of humans. Some sharks are hunted, some are caught in fishing nets, and some are killed by pollution. Scientists are helping save sharks and their habitats.

FACT ...

Some sharks are killed for their fins, which are made into soup.

Scientists put tags on sharks to study how they behave.

You can see some sharks in aquariums.

GLOSSARY

breed To have babies.

cartilage A tough, rubbery material that makes up a shark's skeleton.

cruising Traveling at a steady speed.

filter feeder A shark that swallows water and filters food out of the water through its gills.

fin Part of a fish's body that sticks up from its back, sides, or tail.

flexible Able to bend easily without breaking.

fossilized Describes the remains of a plant or animal that died millions of years ago and has been turned to stone.

gills Parts of the body used by some creatures to breathe underwater.

migration A long journey made by many animals to find places to feed and breed.

pollution Poison or harmful things in an environment.

predator An animal that hunts and kills other animals for food.

prehistoric From a long time ago, before history was written down.

prey An animal that is hunted and killed by other animals for food.

species A group of plants or animals that share similar features.

streamlined Having a shape that can move easily through water or air.

tag A marker or label that is attached to something.

yolk The part of an egg that provides food for the growing baby inside.

INDEX

basking sharks 19
blood 17
blue sharks 12, 20
bull sharks 8

cartilage 10

dwarf lantern sharks 4

eggs 20, 21
eyes 16, 17

filter feeders 18, 23
fins 6, 10, 11 14, 28
food 7, 9, 14, 18–19, 23, 24, 25, 26, 28
fossils 6

gills 11
great white sharks 9, 24–25
Greenland sharks 9

hammerhead sharks 16
hearing 16

leopard sharks 13

mako sharks 4–5, 14
Megalodon 6, 7
mermaids' purses 21
migration 9

pups 20, 21

sawsharks 5
skeleton 10
skin 10, 11
spy-hopping 24
Stethacanthus 6

tail 11, 14, 15
teeth 4, 6, 7, 10, 14, 18, 23, 25, 26
tiger sharks 15, 26, 27

whale sharks 5, 22–23
wobbegongs 13

AMAZING SHARKS

Collector Card

AMAZING SHARKS

Collector Card

AMAZING SHARKS

Collector Card

AMAZING SHARKS

Collector Card

Tiger shark

This deadly shark will eat almost anything, including boat cushions.

SCORE

SIZE: up to 16 ft. (5m)	5
DANGER FACTOR: very dangerous	8
TEETH: 1.2 in. (3cm)	5
CONSERVATION STATUS: at risk	7

Dwarf lantern shark

This pocket-sized shark can only be found in the Caribbean Sea.

SCORE

SIZE: up to 8 in. (21cm)	1
DANGER FACTOR: low	1
TEETH: 0.08 in. (2mm)	1
CONSERVATION STATUS: at risk	7

Basking shark

This huge, slow filter-feeder can jump completely out of the water.

SCORE

SIZE: up to 40 ft. (12m)	8
DANGER FACTOR: low	1
TEETH: 0.08 in. (2mm)	1
CONSERVATION STATUS: vulnerable	5

Whitetip reef shark

A small, common reef shark with a great sense of smell.

SCORE

SIZE: up to 6.5 ft. (2m)	3
DANGER FACTOR: low	3
TEETH: 0.4 in. (1cm)	3
CONSERVATION STATUS: at risk	7